Dragon Tales

Written by Jenny Feely

Illustrated by Roberto Barrios Angelelli

Flying Start
to Literacy®

Contents

Prologue

For thousands of years, people have told tales about dragons – powerful beasts that can often do magical things.

In some tales, the dragons use their power for good; in others, they bring terror and destruction.

Many cultures around the world have stories about dragons. This book tells two tales about dragons: one story is about four very caring dragons, and the other is about a truly terrifying dragon.

Chapter 1
The four dragons
A dragon tale from China

Long, long ago, there were no lakes and rivers in China. There was only the sea, where the Pearl Dragon, the Black Dragon, the Long Dragon and the Yellow Dragon lived.

Living without lakes and rivers was hard for the people of China, especially when it didn't rain.

Without rain, they had no water to drink and little food to eat. Without rain, they could not water the plants that they grew for food, and without water, the plants could not grow.

The Jade Emperor, the ruler of heaven and Earth, controlled the rain. Sometimes, he sent rain and sometimes he didn't.

One day, the four dragons that lived in the sea flew up into the clouds to play.

The Pearl Dragon looked down on the land and saw how dry and brown it was.

The Jade Emperor had not sent rain for a very long time. Days, weeks and months had passed with no rain. The land had turned brown, the crops had died and the people were starving.

The Pearl Dragon called to his brother dragons.

"Look at this!" he said.

"Those people will die if there is no rain soon," said the Black Dragon. "We must help them."

So the dragons flew to the Heavenly Palace to ask the Jade Emperor to send rain.

This made the Jade Emperor angry.

"Why are you out of the sea, where you belong?" he asked.

"We have come to beg you to send rain to the people," said the dragons.

"I will send rain," the Jade Emperor said. "But only if you go back to the sea where you belong – and stay there!"

The dragons went back to the sea and waited. Ten long days passed, but there was no rain.

"We must help the people," said the Long Dragon.

"But how?" said the brother dragons.

"We have plenty of water here in the sea," said the Long Dragon. "Perhaps we can fill our mouths with water and take it up into the sky. Then we can spray it on the land and help the people."

"But what if it makes the Jade Emperor angry?" said the brother dragons.

"It is a risk we must take," said the Long Dragon.

So the four dragons filled their mouths with water. Then they flew up into the sky and sprayed the water over the land.

When the Jade Emperor found out what the dragons were doing, he was very angry indeed.

"I am the ruler of heaven and Earth, and I will decide when it will rain," he said. "Not those dragons."

Now, the Jade Emperor was very powerful. He used his power to imprison the dragons under four great mountains.

The dragons could not escape, but they did not give up trying to help the people.

They turned their bodies into rivers.
The rivers flowed out of the mountains and across the land. The people had water – they were saved.

And this is how there came to be rivers and lakes in China.

The four rivers formed by the dragons still flow through China. The rivers are:

- the Zhu Jiang (Pearl Dragon)
- the Heilong Jian (Black Dragon)
- the Chang Jiang (Yangtze, or Long Dragon)
- the Huang He (Yellow Dragon).

Chapter 2
The Piasa bird
A dragon tale from North America

When European explorers first sailed down the Mississippi River in North America, they saw carvings on the cliffs above the river. The local Native Americans made these carvings long ago.

One carving showed a dragon-like creature. People started to make up stories about this dragon.

In the most popular version and the one that is still told today, the frightening creature is called the Piasa bird (pronounced PIE-a-saw). *Piasa* is a Native American word that means "the bird which devours me".

The original carving that the explorers saw is no longer there. But in the 1800s, some people drew a picture on the same cliffs, based on the early descriptions of the original.

Long ago, in a village on the Mississippi River, people lived happily. Their village was surrounded by cliffs and forests that protected it from harsh winds. The river was full of fish, the forests had lots of animals, and there was always plenty of food.

The chief of the village was Ouatoga. He was very old. When he was younger, he had been a brave warrior. He had saved the village from many wars, and there had been peace in the village for a very long time.

Then, early one morning, as the sun was rising in the sky, terror touched the village.

Some young warriors had set off on an early-morning fishing expedition. As they paddled down the river in their canoes, they suddenly heard an alien scream. The warriors looked up to the sky.

And there they saw something they would
never forget. A huge monster was flying
towards them.

Before the warriors knew they were in danger,
the monster swooped down and carried one
of them away.

No one could agree on what was most terrifying about this creature. Was it the Piasa's body, which was covered with scales? Or its tail, which was long and sharp like a snake? Or its wings that were wider than those of the largest bird?

Perhaps it was its humanlike face, or its long, sharp claws. Maybe it was its huge white fangs.

The one thing that everyone agreed on was that the Piasa bird was terrifying. And the most terrifying thing about it was what it hunted . . . humans.

Every morning, the Piasa bird crawled out of its cave high in the cliffs above the village. It stretched its wings in the sun and opened its mouth to let out a blood-chilling scream. It swooped down from the cliff to hunt for its favourite food. And then it would return to its cave with a victim in its sharp claws.

Fear spread throughout the village.

Hundreds of warriors tried to kill the Piasa bird, but their arrows bounced off its scaly skin.

The villagers went to see the chief.

"You must save us from this dreadful monster," they begged, "before our whole village is destroyed."

"What can I do?" said Chief Ouatoga. "I am an old man, and I am tired. If the young warriors cannot kill this terrible Piasa bird, how am I to do it?"

"If you cannot save us, then we are doomed," the people said.

Chief Ouatoga asked the Great Spirit to help him. He sat out under the sky for 28 nights. The moon grew fat and then thin, and he waited patiently for a sign.

Then, one night, while Chief Ouatoga was sleeping, the Great Spirit answered him.

Chief Ouatoga had a dream. In this dream, he saw the Piasa bird fly high up into the sky. As it flapped its wings, the chief saw that the terrible creature did not have scales under its wings.

This gave Chief Ouatoga an idea. He called together everyone in the village and told them his plan. They sharpened their strongest arrows and dipped the points in poison.

That night, the chief and six of the best warriors crept to the top of the cliff. The warriors hid behind the rocks out of sight with their bows ready. Chief Ouatoga stood on the edge of the cliff. They waited all night.

As the sun started to climb in the sky, they heard a terrible scream. Suddenly, the winged monster swept into view.

When it saw Chief Ouatoga standing on the edge of the cliff, it swooped down and grabbed him with its sharp claws. Chief Ouatoga quickly fell to the ground and held on to the roots of a tree. He could feel the pain from the creature's sharp claws, and this made him hold on even more tightly.

As the Piasa bird flapped its huge wings in an effort to carry off Chief Ouatoga, the six warriors stepped out from their hiding place. Each warrior shot a poisoned arrow into the unprotected skin under the creature's wings.

Again and again the bird flapped its wings to fly away with Chief Ouatoga.

But Chief Ouatoga would not let go of the roots. He held on tight, and each time the miserable creature flapped its wings, the six poisoned arrows drove deeper into the bird's soft skin.

Finally, the poison worked. The Piasa bird screamed in agony and released its hold on Chief Ouatoga.

Down, down, down it fell into the mighty Mississippi River, where it sank like a stone and was never seen again.

The warriors carefully carried Chief Ouatoga back to the village, where he was cared for until he healed.

The next day, the warriors went back to the
cliffs and began the painting of the Piasa bird
so that no one would ever forget the bravery
of Chief Ouatoga and the secret to defeating
the Piasa bird.

A note from the author

I grew up listening to and reading stories about dragons – stories filled with suspense and adventure. Some of the dragons in these stories were fierce and terrible; others were friendly and helpful.

I knew that dragons weren't real, but I loved to imagine what the world might be like if they were.

I still love to read about dragons, but now I am lucky enough to get to write about them, too.

I hope you have enjoyed the dragons in these tales as much as I have enjoyed researching and writing about them.